The Definitive Guide for choosing Business Management Software

(without getting tied down)

You want to change, and you change.

The authors.
To be honest, we have to say that the real authors of this guide have been our clients. They told us, with varying levels of frustration, about the majority of the situations outlined here and they made us see the need to gather information on purchasing or replacing an ERP and compiling it in a format that is useful to other companies considering purchasing such programs.

However, although our clients have been a priceless source of inspiration, we have written and published this guide. Practically everyone who forms a part of NaN-tic has made a contribution to the information provided on these pages. Two people however led the project:

Albert Cervera

This guide was his idea. Albert believed that this type of publication was essential, he decided how it was going to be organised, who was going to make the first drafts and he supervised the project.

Surprisingly, Albert is not a literary editor, but an I.T. engineer with a post-graduate degree in financial management. He is also one of the founding partners of NaN-tic and the consultant for the majority of the company's most important projects. His keen interest in free software has led to his participation in a number of initiatives related to open-source technology. If you are interested in this subject, you may find him speaking at a conference or working as a partner on a major project.

Marc Redorta

Marc has been responsible for organising, writing, revising and translating almost everything contained in this guide.

Marc is a Communications and Marketing Consultant with experience in different companies and projects related to the area of business management software. He has been working with NaN-tic since 2012, and has helped us to position the company and to attain more high-level clients. He has also worked in different administrative organisations, as well as in the national media. And we have to admit, that when it comes to writing, he's not too bad at it.

Index

1 / **If you are reading these words,** it's likely that

you're thinking about installing a new software program for your company. Or you might even have taken this step in the past, and the experience was so unpleasant that you now want to try to understand where you went wrong. Whatever the case, please keep reading.

We decided to write this guide after seeing just how concerned managers and IT professionals were when they came to ask us for advice. The vast majority of them had suffered bad experiences in the past or were worried about problems in the future, and as we like to share what we know, we decided to go over the main mistakes people make when selecting management software, and our recommendations for minimising such mistakes.

And that's what this is: The Definitive Guide for choosing your Business Management Software, which is something like a recipe book that will help you to create a dish you have never seen before, or reduce the most important risks involved, while giving you room to focus and work on your own initiative. Because when it comes down to it, you'll see right away that the main problem is that there is never anyone in the company who really has the experience or training to take a decision like this one. Ignorance about the product and the technology involved leave us at the mercy of salesmen and their persuasive talents, and people often make a decision based on their intuition and not on the real facts available.

And before we begin, just one last thing; don't expect us to tell you which type of software you need. That's not down to us. We'll explain how to deal with the process, what you have to look at and what questions you'll need to ask the sales people, we'll point out the common pitfalls you might find along the way and even how to avoid them. But we've not written this guide to sell you a product. We want to help you deal with the selection process, with information on hand, and without the anxiety and stress of not knowing whether what you're buying is really what you need, and if it comes at the right price.

However, we do want to tell you that we love open source – i.e. software made in a cooperative manner that can by modified and distributed freely, without restrictions

of any sort. It forms part of our way of understanding the world in which we live and work. This is why we also want to use these pages to explain just what these free technologies can offer companies. We want you to see them as another option in the wide range of management solutions available on the market. With this information you'll be free to make an informed decision on what best serves your interests.

2 / SOS I need software!

It's more and more obvious with every new day. When it comes to company management, your business is on the limits of chaos. Daily administration is not systematic. Your clients don't receive the products or services they need on time. Billing is getting more complicated by the day. Tax and regulatory changes involve additional headaches. Information is not centralised. Your sales team are using slow tools, you don't have the information you need to take strategic decisions, you cannot plan resource use properly, your growth forecasts are looking limited, today's technology does not adapt to the tools you purchased years ago. All in all you're losing control of your own company.

And let's face it, selecting an ERP, a CRM or any management tool is a pretty daunting experience. The process will be long and your investment will take months to provide you with any significant returns. Your staff, who will have to use the new system, will reject it from the start, and if that wasn't enough, without the right info, you'll never be sure about making the right decision. You need to select the right product and supplier for the right price, with technology that won't fall short in a few years. Nor do you want a program that spreads itself everywhere. Unless your IT supplier quits on you or retires, you'll never find the ideal moment to look at alternatives.

The temptation to close this guide right now must be pretty big, but hold on a minute, we wrote it for a reason, and remember – nobody said it would be easy.

On the one hand, you need to remember that the number of times that you're going to need to deal with a business situation like this one is relatively small. In fact people rarely ever have to tackle this process and what's more, what with rapid changes in technology, a large part of this experience will be of no use in the future.

And you also need to think about the consequences, what having this new program will mean for your organisation. More often than not, numerous expectations will have been made, a fact that creates an enormous sense of dependence on the product and on the companies providing services, whether in terms of consultancy, training, programming or hosting.

So - **TIP NUMBER 1: Start by forgetting the idea that you'll be able to select a program quickly and get it working in just a few days or weeks.** Not because it's not viable, which it could be, in some cases, but because of future consequences, which are in no way positive.

3 / How do I begin looking for an ERP?

The three most common ways are the following:

a. Tell an it expert that you're looking for an ERP.
b. I've been told there's a great new ERP.
c. I have no idea about which ERP i need.

These three different cases almost always end the same way, i.e. with someone who enters Google and who starts to search for suppliers of these kinds of tools. In the first case, the IT engineer will most probably focus his research using technological criteria. While in the second case, the search will probably begin by looking for a product made by a specific manufacturer who has been recommended by somebody. In the final case, the process will be initiated in a totally random manner.

However the string of keywords entered into the search engine, an act which in recent years has guided our lives, will have a marked effect on the process that is about to begin.

The algorithms that govern Google searches are the best kept secret of the 21st century. Nobody knows exactly how the company researches, indexes and classifies the searches that appear after keywords are entered. However, what normally happens is that those companies that spend more money on paying Google to advertise their websites are more likely to be found.

In most cases, the search process for an ERP begins by entering some of the following words into the search field:

ERP, BUSINESS MANAGEMENT SOFTWARE, MANAGEMENT SOFTWARE, CHEAP ERP, etc.

And the magic of Google (combined with advertiser investment) will provide determined results.

At this point, it needs to be said that no cases have been documented of people who have gone beyond the first search page, even though there are hundreds of

them. Everyone stays with what is shown on the screen right after clicking on the magnifying glass icon. And normally, results are selected from what is seen at first glance, opening the tabs of those entries that match what they're looking for. The first step of the selection process has therefore been made.

The manufacturers and distributors shown on some of these open tabs are much more likely to capture new clients than those who are displayed with a simple link provided by the search engine, and they know it. This is why, if you search using different keywords, the results offered by Google are always the same.

This is probably one of the first and most important errors in the process. Your search for the product that you need must not involve suppliers and sales representatives. Whether you are the CEO of a company or its Head IT engineer, we recommend that you invest your time in gathering information on what is available on the market, and then using this data to create a document. You need to make a list; of 10 products, for example, which are as different from each other as possible, and at the side of each product, list the advantages and disadvantages discovered by people who have installed these programs in their businesses. This means that you will have to browse user forums or read articles in magazines or specialised blogs. This will not be a waste of time, on the contrary, by using this information you will be able to create a list of strong and weak points associated with each product, and this will allow you to have a visual map of the problems and the opportunities awaiting you. And there are more than a few of them.

And now here's **TIP NUMBER 2: Your first search needs to be more rigorous than you think. You need to spend a lot of time; zoom in and forget about manipulative sales messages.** If you do this, you will definitely reduce the chances of making a mistake.

4 / The first names you see – those who pay the most.
That's how it is and we'll prove it to you. You've begun searching and the products of major manufacturers have appeared on your screen: Microsoft (Navision), SAP (Business One), Sage (Murano), Oracle, etc. It's important to put them on your list and bear them in mind, and do this with others that are more 'home-made', which will also come up. However, all of them have one thing in common; they are proprietary programs.

Proprietary programs are what have always been around; Windows, Outlook or Office. These are the programs, the ones with the licence you never looked at or filled in. You know that you cannot legally make copies of these programs. The users of these programs do not look into whether the program does exactly what they want, or if it does something else - that they didn't want (e.g. Microsoft products were found to send user information to the manufacturer without consent).

We buy and install these programs and there are even those that are installed at source. If you want new versions, you normally end up paying for them and if you don't want the new versions, you stop paying and that's that. Take a look at your product licence, let's face it, it's daunting, but it always offers you peace of mind. Although there have been cases where users installed an ERP, thinking that they had bought it, however they were – according to the licence – merely renting the program, which meant paying the additional costs entailed by updates and new versions.

In terms of free software, all of this is radically different. What we call free software or open source programmes are those programs that may be modified or copied freely and legally, as users have access to the source code. We will go into the pros and cons involved shortly, however, by way of introduction, this feature dispels any anxieties you might have when making program copies. With free software, the idea of a 'licence' is totally without meaning. You can copy or install a licence in as many computers as you want, without having to worry about it – and it's completely legal and free.

To explain this in a little more detail, we'll use a **CULINARY METAPHOR.**

You want to change, and you change.

A licence is a set of constraints that the intellectual owner of a product imposes on those people to whom he authorises its use. Traditionally, computer programs have placed severe restrictions on purchasers and users with respect to making new copies or modifying them in order to adapt them to new needs. Many programs are in fact so well-guarded that is impossible to examine them professionally in order to see if they really do what we want them to do.

It could be said that a source code is to software, what a recipe is to a special dish. A chef may decide to do three things to a dish that he has created: firstly, he may decide not to make the recipe public. This means that whoever wants to eat that dish has to go to his restaurant. This would be the case of proprietary programs, which are the most common these days. If you want to use the program, you buy it, but you won't know what it's made of.

However the chef may also decide to explain what ingredients are included in the recipe – this means you can be certain that the dish is not harmful; an act appreciated by those with gluten or lactose intolerance or who are allergic to some foodstuffs. But the chef decides not to disclose the steps followed in the creation of his dish. In IT terms, this would be like a licence that allows us to see the code, but not reproduce it or adapt the program to our own needs.

Finally, the chef may decide to facilitate the entire recipe, so that anyone who wants to make the dish at home or adapt it to their own tastes and needs may do so. In this case the chef can only make a living if he is capable of constant innovation. The dish will not be exclusive, and any diner may decide at any time, to make the dish himself. Perhaps you want to be surprised by new dishes and recipes – in fact the clients at the former number one restaurant in the world "El Bulli" did not go there simply due to the fame of Chef Ferran Adrià, they also went because he was able to surprise them. And the same thing occurs with free software, it's not enough to do something well once and then live off that feat, because everyone can copy it and even improve it, as they will have all the information they need.

And that's the end of the CULINARY METAPHOR, because in reality, things are much more complex. With free software you can find over forty different licences, however they will always have the common factor that the entire 'recipe' is provided and purchasers can use them whenever they want to and adapt them.

The aim of this guide is not to provide a master's degree on licences for its readers; however it is worthwhile mentioning that for those interested, the website http://www.tldrlegal.com features clear, intelligible summaries of the differences and characteristics of a large number of free licences.

The problem is that during the research phase, some of these alternatives, which may be strategically interesting, and which should at least be taken into consideration, do not appear in a browser's preliminary Google search results.

NaN-tic
You want to change, and you change.

5 / Is open source the best?

This is a difficult question to answer, the fact that a program is free or proprietary does not necessarily mean that it is better or worse. There are proprietary programs that are excellent and others that are very bad, and the same goes for open source software. What happens is that free software is usually expressly made with a certain 'disadvantage', especially in the ERP sector.

Proprietary ERPs produced by large-scale manufacturers come with more marketing and more prestige. This means that it is far easier to find someone in the sector who already has a proprietary tool rather than an open source version. Does this make it better? The answer is no. It may sometimes make users feel more confident, especially to the person responsible for its purchase. Our experience has shown us that SAP or Microsoft tools are often bought, not on a basis of surety, but in order to minimise risks; i.e. to avoid criticism from within the company: the purchase is seen to be justified as it is a tool already used by thousands of companies worldwide, even though the cost is far higher and the tool far bigger than they need to be. Here a list of the main pros and cons involved in free software is what is needed:

Pros

• Usually free. You don't have to feel like a crook when you make copies or ask someone to give you a licence code.

• Flexible. You almost never have to deal with more software than you need, nor will you be left wanting. The program can grow with your business.

• Transparent. Nobody can rip you off. Any IT engineer can see how it's programmed and make the modifications you need.

Cons

• Different. Choosing open source may mean having to migrate databases and other elements to this type of technology.

- Minority technology. Even though it is increasingly more popular, there are still setbacks when choosing non-majority technology, especially when it comes to an ERP.

- Accessible. Anyone can play with an open source program, because you can enter freely, with all the risks that this involves.

Having said this, we can now move on to **TIP NUMBER 3: Analyse programs and evaluate them without prejudice and think about benefits for your company.** Then take the decision that seems the most appropriate.

NaN-tic
You want to change, and you change.

6 / Let the consultation begin! And right after TIP NUMBER 3, comes **TIP NUMBER 4: Don't even think about choosing a management tool yourself. Even though it may mean taking up the time of employees and management in the company, listen closely to their opinions and allow them to take part in the final decision.** They will help you more than you could even imagine.

Why is choosing a business management tool so difficult? Because you need to do it once and do it right. An ERP is a type of tool that in theory, will be used by a company for several years at least, especially if the company grows and the program can be adapted to grow at the same pace. It's highly likely therefore that the person tasked with making the choice has never been in this position before – or that the last time he made the choice was so long ago that the experience is no longer a valid source of criteria as both the company's needs and its set up will have changed, and technology even more so, with new solutions and even new business models. You will need help. But obviously, involving the entire company throughout the whole selection process is not recommended. However those parties who, in our experience, must take part in this task are the Area Head, the CIT Manager, the Financial Manager and the General Manager.

The Area Head

If you are thinking about selecting software to cater for the needs of a determined area, you will need to obtain approval from the head of that section. If, for example, the Sales Department requires a CRM in order to manage business opportunities and sales, you will definitely need to take their opinions into account. If you are looking for a tool for warehouse management, it will be essential to know what the requirements of the Warehouse Manager are.

Things become more complex when you need an ERP, as an ERP is a cross-cutting tool that affects practically all company departments: production, storage, distribution, invoicing, accountancy, human resources and many more. The entire sales area and after-sales service department may require (or already use) an ERP or other similar tools. The good news, therefore, is that if you have decided to install an ERP or replace the one you already have, you'll be able to improve performance in practically all your company departments. The bad news is that if you don't take the right decision, everyone will lose out.

The process is therefore the following: you need to take a strategic decision that will decisively affect company productivity, in addition to growth possibilities in the mid and long term. And all those people trying to sell you their product are dealing every day with something you've never dealt with before or, in the best case scenario, you did many years ago.

So, do you still really want to make this decision on your own? If you want to reduce the risks, speak little and listen a lot. Educate yourself as much as you can and above all listen to those who will need to use the program the most.

The CIT Manager

Imagine that you need to buy a car. If there was a mechanic in the family, it would probably be a good idea to ask him for advice. Plus, wouldn't his point of view have some value when taking the final decision? You'd listen to his explanation about the pros and cons of different models, and you'd ask him about the future maintenance of each option. And it's exactly the same when choosing a management tool for your company.

The CIT Manager, and even your IT engineers, must take part in the selection process from day one. In fact, they already know what the best tools are, and not because of the features offered, but because of how they are made. They know which 'engines' function better or worse, which are easier to repair, which use robust, modern technology and which are now outdated.
This is where, in general terms, open source software offers an undeniable competitive advantage: it is completely transparent. Anyone can analyse how the software has been made, right down to the finest detail, and where necessary, modify it to adapt it to their own specific needs. No tricks, no pitfalls, no false expectations.

What's more, you may find that the rest of the company management staff are not able to calibrate the volume of work that adaptations or modifications needed will involve. Perhaps nobody understands the level of compatibility between the different tools that have already been installed. Therefore, the opinion of the Technology Manager, of the 'Head of Mechanics', for example, must be taken into serious consideration, as in the end, these are the people who will have to take part in the installation and implementation of the new program and they will have to harmonise it with your pre-existing software. Ignoring or undervaluing their criteria is an error that may be a highly expensive one.

.The Financial Manager

This figure is usually the 'bad guy' of the film. His work involves the economic monitoring and control of the company and analysing how resources can be optimised. Therefore any new investments might be seen to come at a bad time, or as excessive, or not properly justified. Or all three at once.

You'll need to make an effort and overcome his initial resistance and win him over for the cause. The way to do this is to show him the benefits of the tool you're considering will have for the company as a whole, and for his own job in particular.

An ERP is basically a control system. It involves the unification of data entry, greater tracking capacity, less circuits and internal processes, the ability to improve planning and production, greater capacity for analysis, and ultimately, more and better information on which to base strategic decisions.

However, despite all of this, an ERP costs both time and money. On the one hand it involves an important economic investment that will determine the day to day operation of the company, and even its growth possibilities in the short and mid-term. However on the other hand, it will also require many hours of work in the selection process, during implementation, in the training phase, and finally in adapting to the new system by practically all members of the company who will need to enter data into it. The presence of the Financial Manager in the process is therefore highly necessary.

And now we come to one of the most complex questions: "How much is an ERP?" Although the easiest answer would be "Whatever you want to spend". Open source ERP programs are free. Program cost = 0. While there are also products on the market that are aimed at large corporations, which are highly expensive. Although, this doesn't really mean much. An ERP cannot be installed like a mobile phone app, it requires many hours of IT engineer work, as the program takes information from where it's needed, it processes it as required and then displays it in an appropriate manner; and all this needs to be analysed beforehand, carefully, in order to ensure that unexpected surprises do not arise. Furthermore, it must be integrated with other tools and databases already installed in company servers, migrations need to be made, tests need to be carried out and users need to be trained before the 'launch' – a word which produces both enthusiasm and anxiety in equal measures among those who have purchased the product and those who sold it to them.

And that's not all there is. Purchasing an ERP or a similar management tool has nothing in common with any other purchasing process or service acquirement procedure. Normally, when you buy a program, you are informed about the price and normally the support or maintenance costs, or even the annual program licence renewal costs. But then come the extras. It turns out that the database management system you're using also needs a licence. And this licence might just happen to be renewable too. And maybe when you need new versions of the program, you'll need to renew it with some extras, and so on. In fact, it's extremely difficult to say how much an ERP costs, but it's even more difficult to say how much it's going to cost. In order to avoid misunderstandings, we provide our clients with a list of the associated costs that may be involved in the purchase of a tool of this type. The list may vary from one purchase to another, but in general terms, it looks something like this:

- Annual transfer for new ERP versions
- Client data transfer to new versions
- Transfers for adaptations to new versions
- Obligatory accounting updates
- Free hosting to NaN-tic servers, to the cloud or to the client's own servers
- Total guarantee. Direct resolution of incidents without dependency on the software manufacturer
- Server monitoring
- Updating of the server operating system
- Total access to the code and database
- Backup copies
- Hosting of backup copies on an external server
- Remote connection to client server
- Licences for the ERP user
- Database licences
- Licences for the server operating system
- Citrix licences for remote access
- Licences for monitoring software
- Technician working hours for ERP, data base and server operating system updates.

Not all the extras on the list are compulsory, nor do they necessarily come at a price, but it is essential to establish what they are. You need to ask if each of these items is included in the estimate presented to you, and where this is not the case, ask that these costs be detailed.

NaN-tic
You want to change, and you change.

Therefore, accept that you'll need to assign an annual budget for maintenance of the tool and you will have to put pressure on your supplier so that he provides you a simulation of the annual cost for the purchase and the maintenance of the tool over the first three years, for example.

If the final cost of the operation exceeds your most pessimistic forecasts, you still have two options left open: one – evaluate what phased (gradual) implementation would cost. This means beginning with the smallest possible investment and increasing program use as the financial capacity of your company grows. In this sense, open source software, apart from eliminating all expenses related to operating licences, usually provides greater flexibility too, enabling improved adaptation to changing circumstances. Ask your supplier about the minimum investment you need to launch the system and the implementation roadmap for the coming years.

The other option is to use what is known as SaaS (Software as a Service). You'll lose flexibility, because the program cannot be adapted too much (or hardly at all) to corporate needs, given that it will be installed in an external server (cloud). This option means that you pay a monthly fee for its use and maintenance while forgetting about new versions, licence renewal and other options unattractive to your Financial Manager. The problem is that some potentially interesting products may not be very useful for your company and you will have to eliminate them from your list.

Conclusion: Choosing the right ERP is difficult, but it is even more difficult to guess the impact that it will have on company finances. Ensure that all meetings on this issue include the attendance – and participation – of the Financial Manager.

The General Manager

We'll start off here by assuming that your General Manager is the person who possesses an overall strategic vision of the company. And in a modern company the main tool that helps to make the company work cannot be considered to be a marginal topic. In fact, the selection of one tool or another has a clear strategic component, with respect to how the company plans its actions in the coming months and years. Improving the company in a technological manner, in order to begin exportation is not the same as opening new sales points. Forecasting low-scale, sustained growth is not the same as an important quantum leap resulting from a purchase or an injection of capital.

Having said that, the General Manager often does not have the time (nor often the energy) to follow the entire process closely. Despite this, our experience has led us to recommend that the General Manager should take part in the definition of the basic internal guidelines, that he should supervise the evaluation process of the different alternatives available and be involved in the final decision.

By way of example, here are some questions, which in our opinion should be made by the General Manager in order to make more appropriate decisions:

- Is there any problem with the data being outside the company?
- Is a more expensive, but non-open source option being prioritized, or is emphasis being given to one that is cheaper, but more flexible?
- What supplier profile are you looking for? Brand or close-at-hand?
- Do you prefer to subcontract developments made, or do you trust your own IT staff?
- What economic and contractual links are you willing to accept?

As it can be seen, all the major questions focus on a central point; the relationship with the supplier. It has been said that choosing a supplier, or partner (as they are referred to in the sector) is like getting married. It is an important step that establishes a long-term link, and all too often one that is stronger than expected.

If we insist on the idea that the selection of a tool is a critical moment in the history of a company, it is because you cannot take it back after a few days. And then it will be too late to read this guide. Purchasing an ERP and linking yourself to a supplier must be made from the position of having properly analysed all the viable proposals on the market, and from the conviction that the supplier is honest, open and professional.

Here we need to stress the need to be frank and direct in your negotiations. What sense would it make if you told your supplier that you have severe budget restrictions, if later you give him access to all your accountancy data? What logic would establishing a determined negotiation strategy have if the supplier later enters the company and you tell him how your purchasing process works? What sense is there in requesting assessment from someone when you are unwilling to explain everything to them? A relationship of trust is essential and it must exist for both parties. However good the product is, or the expert's references, if there is a lack of trust, there are major risks. Think about going for a coffee with your supplier, before making a decision you might regret.

Furthermore, you must remember that you will find companies of all kinds during the installation process, from those that document nothing and hardly explain a thing to you, to those who document everything. Here is another important point: the rigorous documentation of requirements does not necessarily guarantee the success of the project. And it is highly unlikely that users understand absolutely all the details of the new tool just by reading a document. There will always be misunderstandings, so a middle way is probably preferable, i.e. to neither begin things without knowing what you're doing, nor wait until you have everything documented before you begin; detailed total documentation would be better for the installer than for the client, as having everything laid out in writing gives him room to say "we didn't anticipate this point".

And here you have **TIP NUMBER 5: When faced with two options without too many economic or technological differences, prioritize harmony and complicity with your program installers and it will be more difficult to make mistakes.**

Xavier Fuertes. The Association of Journalists of Catalonia

« I recommend that when you lead or manage a company, you should ask for expert advice. [...] For us, a strategic inconvenience is being in the hands of a brand or a company or a small group of people who have created a tool that is so important that without it the company cannot even open the front door [...] We are already dependent on these technologies, and therefore avoiding a dual dependency was the main reason I had for recommending that the Association of Journalists opted for open source programs.»
http://www.nan-tic.com/en/xavier-fuertes

You have noted down details, you have selected three or four key staff members who will help you choose the tool. You have defined several strategic aims for the company, which the new tool will help you to attain. The time to decide has come. The distributors are waiting for your call or a mail. But wait, don't be too hasty; read the next chapter of the guide before doing anything else.

7 / 10 Essential questions before choosing your tool

Here's our experience, condensed in ten key questions. When meeting up with potential suppliers, follow this questionnaire in this order, and you'll obtain the information you need to take the right decision.

#1 Does it do what I need?

This probably seems like an obvious question, but you need to ask it. Remember that the answer might not be as simple as you had imagined. Business applications usually come with a wide range of possibilities and different ways of tackling problems. What's more, it's also easy to have too many features. Does the application you're thinking of buying do much more than what you really need? Does this affect the cost or make using it more complicated? Does it affect its performance?

Think, for example about a tool for managing production that requires information to be entered for planning, when this is a need you don't have. You could find yourself having to compile and enter information that will only be used to keep the system 'happy', because it has been made in this way, and not because its real need for the business.

#2 Will it do what I need tomorrow?

Companies evolve and if they don't then something is wrong. The market is dynamic and needs appear constantly. The question is therefore clear; does the tool allow modifications to be made in the future? Will it allow you to grow or will it limit your expansion?

As we've mentioned before, an ERP should be useful for a business for many years. It is therefore highly improbable that in all this time, the company's primary 'motor' will not need adjusting, that no changes will be made in legal regulations (e.g. tax increases), or that no issues relating to production, storage or distribution will be changed. What happens when all of this takes place? What are your options with respect to the tool?

Never buy a program that contains many more features than those that you really need, but never purchase one that will limit growth.

#3 What do annual maintenance costs amount to? What hidden surprises await me?

As you want an ERP and are prepared to pay for it, remember that you'll also want to use it in future years. This means that you'll have to continue paying, despite what some salesmen might try to tell you. Ask for a cost simulation on 1, 3 and 5 years. Find out about costs related to changes of versions, licence renewal, after-sales services, and the training of new users.

Ask about collateral expenses too. Will you need new hardware when you install this new software? Do you need to modify your databases? Do you have to implement or replace an already-existing program? Demand openness and clarity right from the start. You'll need it.

#4 What about licences?

We've already talked about this, but here's an added factor – in the area of proprietary programs, you generally need one licence for each program user. If your company has 30 employees who will need to work with the ERP in one way or another, you will have to take on the cost of 30 licences. And of course, if things don't go as planned, you won't be able to return the licences or get a refund on them, you'll have paid for a whole year; and there's no way out of it.

Evaluating the pros and cons of the licencing system compared to open source programming is a good idea. The latter option will allow you to make as many instalments and acquire as many permits as you want, without any repercussions on software costs. The same goes for the delicate matter of annual renewals.

We earn a good living thanks to clients who are not willing to pay the abusive price demanded for annual licence renewal. We know what we are talking about.

#5 What about new versions?

The updating of versions should be good news for a company, as these are improvements on the original program, however it sometimes seems that they are designed

merely to instigate panic. On the one hand, you should clearly establish as to whether software updates are included in the price, or if you have to take on an additional cost, and on the other hand, you have to hope that any updates do not involve a modification of processes, which up until now functioned correctly. Furthermore, when a new version is available, you need to look at the improvements involved and above all, what adaptations are affected.

Having said this, a slow pace of updates may also be a problem, as it may indicate low levels of program flexibility on incorporating changes and the improvements needed.

Insist on this issue, a salesman needs to explain in detail how this matter is resolved and what resources you will need. If he tells you that you won't need to pay anything, you have every reason to doubt him. There are large manufacturers who only provide technical service to the users of their two latest program versions. The toll, in this case, is high and often hidden.

#6 What's my relationship with the supplier?

Reading the small print is highly unappealing, but changing your supplier is even less attractive, believe me. Because when you change it's a bad sign, it means that you don't get on with your service provider, that you don't believe that their staff are competent enough or that they're not charging you a fair price.

It's also unappealing because it's not necessarily simple. Contracts with suppliers, or partners, for management tools may include hidden clauses that all too often are not explained when the sale is made. There are manufacturers who oblige their clients to pay a yearly fee simply for benefitting from a supplier's after-sales services. Others reserve exclusivity over the installations of new versions. In short, this point needs to be hammered out and defined.

#7 Who gives me support in the future?
Who's going to help me?

Having an ERP is easy, but making it do what we want isn't such a simple task. Taking this premise as a starting point, and in our experience, we can assure you that you'll have to consult your supplier in order to resolve all types of incidents, and often. Some issues may arise at source, others may be unforeseen, due to new needs or regulatory changes. New versions will also emerge that may affect adaptations made previously. This final issue is highly important, because you

cannot avoid it. The scenario is as follows, as your company has several specific needs, you'll be making modifications to the program. However, will these adaptations work when new program versions arrive? Will you need to re-adapt them? And if so, at what cost?

It's a good idea not to underestimate the value of after-sales services, they should even be considered as a key factor when taking your final decision. The questions you need to ask in this point are the following: Who will provide me with support? When I have a problem, who will help me solve it and how? If the incident is due to a program error, can someone resolve it for me? Will the manufacturer shirk responsibility? Never forget that all programs have their errors, and if you are told otherwise, it's because the support you're being offered is either poor quality or non-existent.

To put it another way, not only do you have to seek out a good program, you should also look for a good supplier. Search for someone who you feel you can trust, who is technologically prepared and above all, who understands your business and the way that you work. We also recommend calling some of your potential supplier's clients (use the 'client success story' section on their website) and ask them about the after-sales service they offer. A couple of calls could save you a lot of time and hassle.

#8 Is there a chance of getting a demo version to test?

Imagine that you're about to buy a 25,000 euro car. Would it be wrong to ask about a test drive it beforehand? In reality you're about to purchase software that may cost you two or three times more. So ask for a demonstration. But not one where someone comes along with a computer and shows you a demo version. Ask them to install the program in your computer for a couple of weeks, so that you can try it out and get used to it. You need to have questions to ask, and find out what you like and what you don't. You need to simulate your company's procedures with real data, like how you manage exceptional processes, so that you can check that the program's logic matches that of your company. The idea is that the software should adapt to your needs and not the other way around.

You might find that some sales representatives might not like this idea too much, but insist. There's nothing better than trying out what you're thinking of buying.

#9 Should I get training before buying the software?

This is not a common question, although it is a very important one. Once you're sure about which tool seems to be the best, which adapts better to both your company's current and future needs, we recommend taking a training course with the supplier before buying the program or contracting their services. This is something like a couple living together before they decide on getting married.

You'll not be wasting money with this training course. Firstly, because if the program is the right one, you'll already be trained to use it. Which means you'll be ahead of schedule. But if it turns out that the program isn't the right one, the training will have helped you not to make the wrong decision, which is no small victory. Not marrying the person who isn't for you is a good thing, right? But what's more, you'll have acquired new know-how on the possibilities regarding the types of tools you want to purchase and the technology available on the market. This will allow you to seek alternatives and re-evaluate those which in theory you had discarded before. In all events it's an investment in knowledge that will remain in the company.

Conclusion, take no notice until you are totally convinced, and take note of **TIP NUMBER 6: Take a software training course focusing on the program you think you'll end up buying, but don't take your final decision until you've finished the course.**

#10 Does it respond to my company strategy?

This final question is one that you will have to ask and answer yourself. Once you have the answer to the previous nine questions, you'll have, on the one hand, a lot of information and knowledge, on the other, you'll have a lot of salesmen hysterically pressuring you to buy their products.

It's time to take the decision. The tool needs to resolve your current and future needs, and therefore responds to a business strategy and philosophy. Think about the management model that you want for your company and which of the programs you evaluated responds best to this idea. Also check if the tool can resolve the aims you established initially, or if in the meanwhile you've gone 'off-track' and are no longer thinking about the problems you have to tackle in the real world.

NaN-tic
You want to change, and you change.

8 / Time to decide

Well, here you are, finally at the end of the process – and one that seemed almost impossible to start with. Now, if everything has gone smoothly, you should have a clearer idea about the type of program that you need and which program you are going to buy. You should also know who you are going to buy it from.

You will have listed the names of manufacturers and distributors, analysed present and future needs, compared technology and business models. You will have met friendly representatives and others with whom you wouldn't share a lift with. You should be able to detect potential pitfalls and hidden links and you will have seen outrageous and widely differing prices.

You'll have shared this process with some of the company team. The time has come to make the decision. You should now have all the information at your disposal to do this.

So take a sheet of paper and note down the pros and cons of the two or three products that have passed through the selection process to the finals. Explain the details to your colleagues and outline the arguments in favour of the product and the distributor that you propose. Finally, if everyone agrees on the decision, call the sales rep and make his day.

NaN-tic
You want to change, and you change.

9 / Important advice

Tip number 1: Start by forgetting the idea that you'll be able to select a program quickly and get it working in just a few days or weeks.

Tip number 2: Your first search needs to be more rigorous than you think. You need to spend a lot of time; zoom in and forget about manipulative sales messages.

Tip number 3: Analyse programs and evaluate them without prejudice and think about benefits for your company.

Tip number 4: Don't even think about choosing a management tool yourself. Even though it may mean taking up the time of employees and management in the company, listen closely to their opinions and allow them to take part in the final decision.

Tip number 5: When faced with two options without too many economic or technological differences, prioritize harmony and complicity with the program installers and it will be more difficult to make mistakes.

Tip number 6: Take a software training course focusing on the program you think you'll end up buying, but don't take your final decision until you've finished the course.

You want to change, and you change.

10 / Glossary

All too often, business management software experts use a language that is as commonplace to us as it is exotic to those outside the field. We use technical expressions or highly technical terms that are unfamiliar and which may lead to confusion. This guide would not be complete without a brief glossary of terms that are usually used when selecting a tool of this sort. We have included our own here in order help with doubts and clear up certain concepts.

The terms below are, in our view, essential to this subject matter:

Business one. This is the flagship SME management product of the German company SAP. It is a proprietary program that is sold with the traditional system of licences and which is widely used by numerous companies.

Cloud. The cloud, or cloud computing is a new way of offering computer services that is based on Internet access or to a data network. The idea is that technology is hosted and centralised in external servers and that the user pays to access them using the Internet. This saves on maintenance and hardware expenses and means that a company only has to pay when it uses the services it requires.

Consulting. The process of installing an ERP in a company always involves a primary assessment phase. The aim of this process is to properly diagnose the real needs of the company and the expectations of its managers in order to be able to successfully carry out programming and software implementation.

CRM. Customer Relationship Management is the tool venerated by any marketing department. It facilitates the control, analysis and management of all business opportunities, in addition to relations with already-established clients. Its integration with the ERP is essential in taking strategic decision in the area of sales.

Database. According to Wikipedia, a database is a collection of data organised in a coherent structure that is accessible from one or more programs or applications. In short, it is to an ERP what petrol is to an engine. Having well-stored data is the first step for the correct and efficient management of a company.

E-Commerce. Everyone knows what e-commerce is, but everyone asks us how online sales platforms are related with ERPs. Each case needs to be studied; however we believe that the highest level of integration is needed in order to provide the highest level of development in respective software programs. In all events, you should know that the most popular e-commerce solutions in the world have been developed using open source programming.

ERP (Enterprise Resource Planning). This entire guide concerns ERP programs, which facilitate business management. The general idea of the guide is to explain how to deal with the complex process of selecting tools of this type.

Free *software*. We have dedicated an entire chapter to free or open source software. We have listed its pros and cons and we have looked at the business models around this philosophy. In brief, this software may be used, copied or modified without restrictions of any type. It is free to use and anyone can look into how it has been constructed and modify it as they see fit.

Implantation. Installing an ERP isn't like downloading a mobile phone application, it requires hours of planning and programming before reaching this point, which is when it is installed in the company's hardware. It is a delicate moment that, if not undertaken professionally, can take nervous breaking strain to the very limit. You need to trust in a chosen supplier and assume that later adjustments will always be necessary.

Licence. A word both feared and loathed by users of proprietary programs, as it is the synonym of charging money for the right to individual program use. However, for those of us who defend and recommend the use of solutions based on open source programs, it is completely inoffensive.

Navision. This is another example of a widespread proprietary ERP, in this case manufactured by Microsoft. We could say that it is a classic in the sector, with a large number of users around the world, as it was launched on to the market in the mid- 1980s. Even though it allows more personalisation than other solutions, such as SAP, the aggressive policy of Microsoft with respect to licences, means that the program is losing its market share to tools in open source.

Open ERP/odoo. This is one of the most popular business management solutions in open source format. In fact we began recommending and installing this solution, however the lack of development planning in the mid and long term and the release of new versions, combined with the appearance of new, opaque links left us, and its users disenchanted. We now recommend Tryton to our clients (see the last point in this glossary).

Partner. This is another word for 'distributor', however in the world of management software the word 'partner' is used. As we have already explained in previous pages, it is essential to establish a climate of mutual confidence before installing an ERP.

Programming. Programming is how IT engineers earn their living, and especially those who work with free software and who do not sell product licences. We mainly develop everything and anything that clients ask us to in order to maximise the use of a new program. A lot of the work involves integration with databases or with already-existing programs in the company. We also carry out adaptations to new versions and deal with unexpected needs.

SaaS. Is closely linked to cloud computing. In fact, it is the result of hosting technology in external servers. It is the acronym of *software as a service* and the idea is to host data and technology in the cloud and use it in accordance with our needs, as a service rather than as a product. This saves on maintenance and other associated expenses.

Training. Training is another important step in the process of setting up an ERP. It is almost always carried out at the end of the process, once the program has been launched, when users need to be informed of how to work with it. However in this guide we place a great deal of emphasis on the need to plan prior training courses, aimed at those with the responsibility for deciding which tool to purchase and install. This will ensure a thorough understanding of product potential and will minimise risks involved in the decision-making process.

Tryton. Is our choice of ERP. It is a robust, transparent, flexible and open product that we recommend to our clients and on which we construct their business plans (as well as our own, obviously). Technologically it is at the same level or even above solutions mentioned in this glossary. It is worthwhile bearing in mind.

11 / Annexe

Some considerations regarding open source programs that we don't want to leave out of this guide. Because, to be frank, open source software creates a certain amount of distrust. Three recurring questions arise regarding our business area that need to be answered.

Are open source programs reliable?

Several years ago the image of open source software was not at its best. It was seen to be something that IT engineers who worked for large software companies did in their free time. The products appeared to be alternatives that in no way amounted to competition for standard programs. We say 'appeared' because many programs revealed an initial robustness that many proprietary programs would have envied. However, one has to make a major act of faith in order to confide in programs of this type, in which barely a single euro has been spent on marketing.

Fortunately things have changed. And we can attest to this. Free software is no longer something weird and is now commonplace in our lives. Popular operating systems for mobile phones and tablets, such as Android or Firefox OS, browsers such as Chrome, Firefox or Safari or the Macintosh printing system are examples of solutions that have been either totally or largely developed using free software and which are used every day by millions of people around the world. To put it another way, it is actually difficult to find someone today who does not have a tool that has been developed using open source programs.

There are of course other, more renowned examples, such as OpenOffice or LibreOffice (office software suites that are highly compatible with Microsoft Office), GIMP (an image editor), Wordpress (the CMS on which most web pages are built), SugarCRM (a business opportunity manager) or the most important e-commerce shops. In some areas, free software is the only program format that has been installed. Good examples are Magento and Prestashop, which are tools for constructing online shops that have become the real winners in this sector, one in which few proprietary programs are used.

NaN-tic
You want to change, and you change.

Apart from these widely-used tools, it is worthwhile mentioning that the computer infrastructure of companies such as Google, Facebook, Twitter and several banking organisations use free software a lot. It is therefore evident that open source is now no longer merely simple entertainment for IT buffs. It is a way of understanding software that is changing industry paradigms at all levels and we are therefore looking at products that are extraordinarily reliable.

One final note: according to the CENATIC Observatory (a Spanish public organisation), 91% of Spanish CIT companies use open source programs in one way or another.

> **Quim Gil, Wikimedia**
> _____
>
> «"I believe that these days we are leaving behind the situation in which, by default, you have to buy licences and if you want to use free software you have to explain yourself to the Board of Directors. Today any 'regular' innovative company in America has to explain why it has had to pay a licence for something.»
> http://www.nan-tic.com/en/quim-gil

Where does free programming come from? How is it made?

Free programming is an open, transparent, accessible phenomenon. But who makes it, and how do the people who invest their time in it earn their livings?

There's possible no other sentence that frightens potential open source users more than "There is no company that manufactures this program". The immediate reaction is to place open source in the mental space for things that are of no interest and which may entail more problems that solutions. "Who do I turn to if there's a problem? Who do I complain to?" are often the questions asked.

But think about it like this: imagine that you had an unknown illness and that you needed medical attention, what would you prefer? Having all your medical history on hand and being able to select the doctors of your choice, or going to the only clinic where they have your information on file? An IT engineer is like a doctor for computers, and when he has access to the source code he will always have resources with which to try and cure the patient. On the other hand, being a captive in the only-available clinic is a little more worrying.

But we'll leave the medical metaphors out of this for a while and focus on the panic-inducing sentence. It's true that behind many open source products there is no single manufacturer. There are usually many experts with many different viewpoints. Open source is made via cooperation and not competition. This means that the improvements requested by a client to his IT specialist or supplier can be used immediately in another location, and without any restrictions.

All of the above translates into the fact that everyone is interested in developing the program and improving it constantly – and even from different starting points. The result is usually a livelier form of software, which has been designed by IT engineers with radically different viewpoints and who have responded to hundreds of challenges put forward by users around the world. We could say that it would be highly difficult to find RDI computer labs that provide better results than those offered by open source software.

How do free software companies make a living?

Investing your time in something you then give away doesn't seem like the best business plan in the world. This is why many people ask us about the business model behind open source. They often ask us "How do you make money?" It's a reasonable question. And more so when there are companies who use free programming as a commercial gambit rather than as a professional philosophy.

But the truth is that there are many possible business models to choose from in the realm of free software. We'll take a look at the most important to understand the type of suppliers you might come across if you choose a tool of this type.

Example 1: A company or professional that creates or improves a product
You need a lot of time, knowledge and experience, but there are many examples of people and companies who make a living from having developed an open source program. Up to this point the business makes no profit, however later, these people offer services, normally in the development of the product, either because their clients want specific improvements or product development.

This normally includes freelancers or very small companies. Some examples are as follows:
Emweb,(http://www.emweb.be); a small Belgian company. They are the creators of a highly interesting tool called Wt (http://www.webtoolkit.eu), which is used for creating web applications in C++ and Java programming languages.

Richard Stallman: apart from being one of the main proponents of free software on a worldwide level, also created a text editing program called Emacs, and he earned his living charging for the improvements requested by some users. The program is widely used and in proportionate terms he had few commissions.

Example 2: Cooperation between various service companies

This is a development of the previous case. Due to the nature of the product, instead of having a single person or a small company that profits from the ecosystem created by a program, several people or companies do so instead. In one way or another they cooperate in the project, they share the costs of maintaining it among each other and they earn a living by offering product-related services to other companies.

Tryton is a good example of this model. Tryton is an ERP, a business management program that is mainly promoted by the Belgian company B2CK, although companies also actively take part in making it grow, thanks to the demands made by their clients.

Just to be clear on this point, this is how we make our living.

Example 3: Foundations that manage resources

This section focuses on larger projects. Here the interests of large companies play a part, and which, unlike the previous cases, these businesses do not earn money directly from the program or the services provided with respect to the program in open source. A well-known example is the Firefox OS operating system for tablets and mobile phones. This free software has been developed by the Mozilla Foundation, which receives money from companies that are far from dedicated to charity, such as Movistar.

More examples are the Apache Foundation, which as in the case above, maintains numerous applications, or the Document Foundation (which is behind the office software package LibreOffice), in addition to the Eclipse Foundation, the Python Foundation and many more. Needless to say, not only are there often large companies that finance foundations, there are also individuals who donate, and participate in their work, as satisfied users.

Example 4: Creating a free version and a private version so that users can decide. Up until now we have talked about free software without limitations, but when companies want to focus on developing open source programs and experience significant growth, they are faced with the incompatibility of combining both.

How can growth be attained if what you produce is sold freely on the Internet?

The solution is not altogether original, but some companies have opted to make use of open source software as an advertising gambit, while offering a 'better' option that is not free. The usual case involves creating a 'Community' version of the program, which is free. Forums are then normally enabled so that developers can make contributions, however, in reality, it is difficult to include changes made by people external to the manufacturing company.

Apart from the Community version, they also offer the Enterprise version (or any other name like this), which includes more features, so that those users who want these improvements need to pay for them, and normally the licence is not free. It must be said that in many successful projects, the Community version is widely used and only very large companies opt for the Enterprise version. There are many successful companies with this model.

Here are some examples:

JasperSoft: an editor of various integrated Business Intelligence solutions with a well-established track record.

Pentaho: as above, they also offer a complete and integrated Business Intelligence solution and have been on the market for many years now.

OpenBravo: this is a company with Catalan capital that has created an ERP (a business management tool). They offer a free Community version, although it is relatively limited, so that some areas, such as production, are payment-based, with a proprietary licence. Users may use the code, but cannot redistribute it, nor therefore improve or reduce long-term expenses. Is this free software? Put it this way; is a vegetarian who eats a barbecue every weekend really a vegetarian?

Magento: is one of the most-utilised e-commerce solutions at a global level. The basic version is free, open and anything you want, but if you want certain extras you need to pay.

Example 5: Selling software that is almost free

There is also the case of companies that have decided not to use these two versions and have opted to increase client loyalty with certain methods that are not altogether clearly defined.

This is the case of OpenERP, which offers the program free of charge, but when you want to move on to the next version of the program, there is no process available that allows this, which means that either you develop it yourself (which is practically impossible and not at all practical) or you pay OpenERP to do the work for you.

In this case the company takes advantage of one of the main errors committed by companies when selecting a management tool: not taking product development into account, i.e. not calculating expenses for software maintenance and evolution over the years.

Example 6: Dual licencing

The last example of a free software business model is that of the dual licence, and it may be the most difficult one to explain, as it is usually adopted by companies that offer their solution to other IT-based companies.

In this scenario, the company develops a totally free-to-use product, however it retains intellectual property rights over it. This means that it can offer the program with a free licence while also offering it with a purchase-based licence. Some types of free licences oblige those users who make program changes to redistribute the program with these changes if and when they redistribute it. This means that those companies that wish to focus on making proprietary programs cannot use the free program as a starting point.

Dual licencing means that manufacturers can offer programs that are both totally open and free to anyone who uses them, with the rules of free licencing, while those who wish to use them, modify them and charge their own licence fees to clients must pay the manufacturer. This allows consumers to choose which rules of the game they wish to follow; free or proprietary.

It is complicated, but some people have managed to earn a living from this model.